"Steadily, unshrinkingly, David Lloyd's *The riarm Fields* confronts the harsh outlines of what remains after atrocity. Tenderly, these poems sound out the dividedness of diasporic being. Historic wounds, here debrided, are opened to air, water, and lapidary attention."—SARAH HAYDEN, author of *Curious Disciplines: Mina Loy and Avant-Garde Artisthood*

"Over the past four decades, David Lloyd's poetry has garnered many admirers—readers drawn to its formal innovation, its wit and intelligence, and its controlled yet deeply committed political engagements. . . . The sheer inventiveness of this now considerable oeuvre—one that is disorientating and exhilarating in equal measure--has few analogues in recent Irish poetry." —ALEX DAVIS, author of *A Broken Line: Denis Devlin and Irish Poetic Modernism*

"People will say it is difficult, but it has a true, necessary difficulty. There is, I think, an overall sense of loss, disappearance, absence. But what really strikes me is a certain kind of consciousness or being which negotiates the physical and the human equally. Someone said of Merleau-Ponty, I think, that he found ways of expressing the human in physical terms, but here the reverse is true too. So, yes, lyric, I think, but not as it is usually construed." —GEOFFREY SQUIRES, author of *Abstract Lyrics and Other Poems*

OTHER PRAISE

For *Under Representation: The Racial Regime of Aesthetics*

"If there is any hope for the human, and if the idea of the human is of any use to the enactment of that hope, then the aesthetic claims and categories through which the human and its subjects are exalted and degraded must be placed under the most violent and most loving scrutiny. *Under Representation* exemplifies such scrutiny. The rigorous care with which David Lloyd examines and challenges the entanglement of race, representation, and the aesthetic is irresistible and indispensable. Under Representation is a major, and singular, achievement."—FRED MOTEN, New York University

For *Beckett's Thing: Painting and Theatre*

"This highly original constellation of critical dialogues will galvanise Beckett studies. David Lloyd both disturbs and enhances emerging debates in and among philosophical, ethical, aesthetic, and political discourses, as they respond to pressures arising from neoliberalization on understandings of human subjectivity and its representability. This book reconfigures how Samuel Beckett's work will be seen and read across a range of fields of enquiry."—VICTOR MERRIMAN, Edge Hill University

the harm fields

GEORGIA REVIEW BOOKS
edited by Gerald Maa

the harm fields

poems

DAVID LLOYD

The University of Georgia Press
ATHENS

Published by the University of Georgia Press
Athens, Georgia 30602
www.ugapress.org
© 2022 by David Lloyd
All rights reserved
Designed by Rebecca A. Norton
Set in 10 / 14 Garamond Pro

Most University of Georgia Press titles are
available from popular e-book vendors.

Printed digitally

Library of Congress Number: 2022936171
ISBN 9780820362625 (paperback)
ISBN 9780820362632 (ebook)

Der Krieg wird nicht mehr erklärt,
sondern fortgesetzt.

—Ingeborg Bachmann

Contents

the harm fields

Leavings

I

Begin to write where there is nothing left to say, only the charge to say it. What a blue sky above the open city, an east wind ruffles the canal. The last ice we hope is parting from the shore with an occasional crack. Two swans take off eastwards, for a time their dangling paddles trouble the water with a wake of silver rings. Whatever it was, I haven't found it here. They drowned Rosa Luxemburg somewhere in this canal. For only too long now some scruple has kept me from writing, for fear the details don't attain to sufficient universality. A—a—a, ah ahah, don't, a, a a a don't worry about your size, said Michael with uncanny insight. His stammer was not debility; he shied away from me on the stair out of a diffuse anxiety, a nervous twitch running down from his right eye through his shoulder. He had the look of a furtive hunchback, though it was just his lurch under his long blue coat. I thought at first it was a harelip but Paddy maintained it was just a slight scar from the night they'd beaten him for kicks behind the pub. Now he never went there any more, but dipped in hurried raids into pubs all over Bethnal Green for never more than a bottle, or came to drink a carryout with us in the house. Paddy figured it must have been after one of the bigger bombings, but probably any excuse would have done. Every emigrant is representative human. The lip was a mere disfigurement. They'd buttoned it for him right and proper. His broken ribs had healed, but their toe-caps had smashed his spine at several points and damaged some motor nerves. So Paddy said at any rate and that was why he couldn't work. Every utterance was a long drawn out stammer from his throat followed by a gabble issuing in a flurry from the front of his mouth. Then a silence, illustrated by a succession of crooked smiles and nods while he waited to see if you had understood. He always meant more than he could say. Or said less than he would. Every motion was a lurch. I never knew if Paddy was Paddy's real name or just the one he went by on the sites. I don't know why he came to the house so often but I hope he found what he was looking for. Sometimes he would help with the building work, but that was mostly just to show he knew more about the business. And that was mostly true. Come spring the community began to break up, since most of us were only wintering out there, exchanging our labour for a bed and some pocket money. They called me Irish too, from time to time, though they often wondered why I didn't have the accent. I suppose that all I had in common with Paddy and Michael was leaving: that's how you get to have a nation. I know no sight more beautiful than Dun Laoghaire fading behind the mailboat. Then it is Bray Head, Killiney Hill and Howth merging with the mountains above the sinking shoreline. Seeing it fade, you start to love it. And everywhere you seek resemblances, or rather, they strike you, and then you realize you were looking for them. Like the canal I always thought must be the swanny river Mrs. McCloskey used to sing about, taking me into town on the bus. It's true, they are alike, and carry you away. Sometimes I think I only know my home by these resemblances. Accentless, you find your refuge in another tongue. There you are far enough and merge with the others. That's the allure of distance: what you never were, you speak, as if the border were a borrowed skin.

I open the journal and it's my mother's face staring sidelong at me
out of Con Markievicz's photo, pistol in hand. As if the eyes were
turned slightly in shame at this assumed relation who was always
disavowed. I miss the figure of the major, her father, he would have
bowed stiffly, taking from her the surrendered pistol, cousins face to
face, with downcast eyes. One dutiful, one a rebel. Both dead before
I knew them, but sometimes it seems the tenor of his voice insists,
petulant, imperious. And I wonder at times if he wasn't the pattern
of those voices ringing out across the bay, over the dunes, at Portnoo
or at Rosbeg, voices my father named for me: "born-to-rule voices."
Later I would find it strange, that he should have given me the words
to scorn them with. The wireless tuned to the Home Service, fuzzy at
times as if the signal dipped below the mountains. Soft, I would say,
a soft egg, trying to find the way to say it so they wouldn't mock me
any more. Years later, two of us met on a station platform, maybe it
was Aix, or Avignon. He had a tricolor on his rucksack. Yes, I said,
yes, I'm Irish too, and, almost, I was born there. Is that right, he said,
is that right? I thought you were English. I see him now stepping
away onto the moving train, heading northwards, fading along the
narrowing tracks. My grandfather spent his last years above the grocery,
my mother must have been bidden to tend to him. She never spoke
much of those things. The last unmarried daughter, except for her twin
Nancy whom I grew to fear. Her tongue clumsy in her mouth, she sat
in the front seat beneath the midland trees, her mug shaky in her hand,
my mother holding the wooden spatula they'd given her, in case the
fit came on. Funny, how she always seemed happy, when we came to

visit, when she visited, her tongue lolling a little, saliva wiped quickly from her chin. Doubtless we all stared. I don't recall, I only remember her fingers tapping time on the aluminium deckchair to some nursery rhyme on Children's Hour or to the signature tune of Women's Hour. The programmes we listened to daily, over lunch. Are you sitting comfortably? Then I'll begin. She had bobbed hair, a little lank and unwashed, her eyes never stood still. My mother's twin. I never could see a resemblance. And yet, if I remember right, it must have been spring, we were walking down towards Hume Dudgeon's stables to meet my sister, and it was my mother teaching us the numbers. One of the happy moments, as I recall, maybe my brother was in his pram, but we sang out as we walked, if I remember right: a-hain, a-doe, a-tray, a-kather, a-cooig, a-shock, a-shay, the rest escape me. Lisping in numbers. The road dips and turns, if I remember right, the architect's modernist bungalow dominating the bend. I left on the ferry and come back by plane. Sometimes I think the language that I never learnt still weighs on my tongue, thickening my Ts behind my teeth.

III

It's not the leaving that's grieving me, but the woman in white waving forlornly at the casement. Remember our descent in May and the white flourish of the blackthorns against the green, how the cloud sheared and reviled with the thrill of returning where you've never yet been. These are the three sorrows of displacement: the song clipped off before its ending; a voice that pauses, uneasy, at the sill; the fall of the rain that's not the same, falling thicker and faster, rinsing a different air; sorrows like an unwarranted rap on the door when another was, well, almost expected. Over and over, one little step more than anticipated, so that even your walk takes on a different gait, cut to another dressage, full of precaution and reserve. Hence this homesickness for places that were never yours, reserves screwed down and slipped sideways out of address. As you speak you speak awry; as you recall it's out of kilter quite. So I feel my heart leap over Shannon or at the bars of "Dear Old Donegal," or sniffing the Liffey air from off the quays. But the name of our hill escapes me still. Cattygollaher, Mrs. McGarry called it over the Sunday papers and a brown bag full of tomatoes. Carrickgolligan in the Ordnance Survey Map of Rathmichael and Environs. I search the buses and the street signs for analogies and come up with Carraig: Bóthar Carraig Bán, Carraig Dubh, Trá Carraig Bán. And at once I'm reclining in bracken under the dome of Golligan's Rock, the Irish Sea blue through the pines, the city looming like a spillway to the north, Bray Head to the south: no sight more beautiful in my recollection. Whoever Golligan was, or was it Gilligan, or MacGillycuddy—MacGillycuddy's Rocks—it's his old man's voice I hear, gravelly and resinous, and again it's a backwash of resin over shingle that I'm thinking of, those voices on the ferry, coming to me off the strings. Hill of Lamentation, says Randolph. Or Massacre, says Louise.

Rock

I

The one who returns returns in
the expectation of exile: is turned
at the slant of light, the door ajar
after all, after the span of freighted years.

As if out of the weight of the rock, its
gravity, at a stroke, a voice and a figure
meld like waters, strange almost as a clearing.

In the distance this sound of a train
drawing away and for a moment
the oldest sound in your world:

                                  a granite duct
siphoned off into the green track, into
the hardness of things, the fears and the leavings:
dust films a haze light cuts a door in

II

The die is cast, and out of that test the things
fall out as they only will. The effects
are haywire, as in the criss-cross play of light
and breeze and ripple across the dock.

Alight on the sand pack alert
for the rock, rock or a constellation:
each one is one yet we name them
fish flash, star light, snatches

off the back of the spume as if there were
airs abroad, *o my grief on the sea* or *my
calling is to the ocean*, the one pacing
along the salt pocked strand, scattered

broadcast as it happens: take with you only
this sweet rain smattering across the salted sea

Kodalith

where to? said a voice then
the voice went away, by which (as if)
time, in a sea a dark mood,
over the rocks, where there are
no rocks finishes you.

—Maurice Scully, *Livelihood*

FIELDS

So livid a gleam along the rim.
White winds descended from the
Shattering fields, runnels groove
The mantle, the folded slab breaks
Down the gradient. Numbed
In the song they sing, lay down
The possibilities: flesh knits its
Meshes into the grain of the stone.

DRYWASH

Dead wind off the fang-range.
Strange weather, strange witness
In the teeth of it, bit and
Grit in the fantail. Did you
Think we would leave and not leave
Bone in the downdrift?
Degrading, silting, grit angel
Sweeping the wash with your wing

PETROGLYPH

Skin burrs. The thumbs impress
The fibres finding the grain
Of the stone. Such transfer,
The light writing turned ghost-
Flesh mapped in stone: did we
Remember the gifted one, the four
Staves of its opening? Nothing
Is given. It gives and is gone.

FACE

What the rockface encloses:
My skin imprinted with
Its warm relief, sugar-
Lift pockmarks. Open
The stone book: light etches
Its ridges, the furrow archive
Sanded away. Scar tissue stares
Into the tender slate.

MANTLE

Rock breaks the living. The living
Wrap stone with all their new
Brutalities: root, blast, frack.
In the breaker's yard, bodies
Bend in the wind. We rattle
Their bones in the crown of
A hat. We rattle. We raffle
The mantle. It shears like
A sea on the shore of the living.

SPINE

Januarized runnels bear down,
Open back into this thing they
Carry forward: acrid taste of
Burnt treacle or some other
Unworldly afterglow. Failed
Wings at the shoulder shrug
Pain to the floor, it slips down
From the spine. Easy. Easy on.

CASKET

Hurt bleeds into another's rib,
Another beat, a casket
Sealed into the cleft for
Future incubation. Lidless
Eye turned in to the handprint
Fixed in sand: night compact
Pressed into the socket. Think it
A fold, a wrinkle, graved in the skin.

SALT

Salt ventures underfoot: a thread
Trodden back into the slab, dulled
Savour to the tongue, reminding.
A plain wind dresses the stone,
Histories scored into its face
It stands out from the dark room,
White remnant of the promised
Flight: what you do give to be of

VITRUVIAN

Vitruvian, ridiculous, braced
In the crevice, the aperture
Shrinks your horizon: black
Marble curtains for you, for you.
Quartered in stone, water-drawn,
Hacked into with light piers,
The white bits ciphered across
The slab. Percussed. Sprung.

PRISM

A thing breaks beyond naming.
In the grit depot, in the shingle
Archive, blood meets with its
Congealing. Your debrided palm
Greets the horizon: sky-prism
Shredding the lightface late
Into the farness, into the violet
Wash over fracture and fold.

COPESTONE

The coping weighs on his shoulder:
Turn at a stroke, to the eyeball
Welled up with minding. What if
The thing should sing then, sing
Out from the nought rim, spelling
With numbers, a jabber flush to
The finish. You're history. Drapes
Sweep the place of its leavings.

CHAMBER

Some pause and then resume. Erratic
Rock adrift on the mantle: what
Are you doing here, stone chamber
Voided with stone? The burden
Bears down on the bone, shin
Ache, joint skew: come dance
With me into the black site, come
Sing with me into the dry dark, into
The wind's teeth, ad lib, ad lib, ad lib

Arcanum

For Fred Moten and Wu Tsang

You step up into the white box. Outside the white box, imagine
yourself a black box. The white box is the inside of the black box.
Suppose each white wall the screen on the outside of a black box, an
arcanum waiting to be inscribed. Who knows how deep this black
box extends unseen this thing that encrypts itself. Once you are in the
white cube, far is as far as you don't see. It knows no outside but the
black box it is inside.

You stand forth against the white walls of the white box. Your shadows
stand forth against the white walls of the white box. Imagine the lights
dim to dark. Then imagine the lights dim to pitch dark. No shadow
no projection no standing forth. Inside the white cube is a black box
unlit invisible. Breathe in you live breathe out you expire. This is the
only sound you would hear. Every other gone.

A white cube has four corners. That goes without saying. A white cube
has a square floor. Beneath notice. A black box stands out at every
corner. Out of one corner a voice says: step up into the square. Circle
the square. The square floor is a public square. We circle the public
square, the cube our quad now. Standing there, already you have
entered the square you circle others circle. This is a circulation without
a center. Were there a center we would not circle. At the center is this
thing we circle and circle.

The thing is a voice. The thing is two voices meeting, passing. The voice is a thing. The voices passing, weaving, are the thing we circle. Into the black box the voice spoke, encrypted. Out of the black box, the voice speaks, circulating. The voice speaks out of its place into this place, this public place. The voice makes the public square, circling the room. Doom. Boom.

Without the body there would be no voice. With the body the voice would be no more. That is its doom. The voices speak from afar. The voice is on the line. The voice speaks in the other's ear. The voice leaves the body the voice circles the voice comes back to you. Disembodied the voice speaks, squared, divided, displaced. Into your body the voice comes, dividing displacing devising. Through the portals, pouring.

We circle the room. At the heart of the room there is no one. At the heart of the room the voices meet. They pass. Out of the abundance of the heart the tongue speaks. Boom. Boom. Out of the quickness of the tongue the heart beats. Boom boom. Who is in love and love replenishes. Who is in love divides the fullness of the body. That is our doom. The voice is a thing we sing.

The heart is a strong muscle. The heart is a circle squared by chambers. The heart is a black box. The heart is a public square. We circle the heart of the matter. The heart beats at the heart of it. The voice skips a beat and we circle the center we miss. Here there and not here. Hear and mishear. Circle the public square.

After Akhmatova

"Why is our century worse than any other?"
—Anna Akhmatova, 1919

after the worst of centuries

a worse

already

ash and blood

on the brow

when the laugh of an American

is an atrocity

when freedom flaps on every screen

as the skin of a wound

flaps

Psalm

I

A corpse is a sudden thing:

You with the litter

        in your white grip

tip this smashed child-thing

        upright into the pit

its rigorous finger

        pulls back the skies

hell flies from

II

Bitter wine of Qana and this is not the end
bitter wine stamped out in the fury of the feast
bright plumes of phosphor seeding iron in the earth
kneading the grain of bodies in with the angry clay
olive trees upended in the fractured soil
bitter wine of Qana and this is not the end

Bitter blood of Qana and this is not the end
the twisted olives with their grey leaves wasted
obstinate dwellings shattered from the hills
bodies scattered beneath the broken bridge
charred beneath the ashes in the narrowest place
bitter blood of Qana and this is not the end

Bitter ash of Qana and this is not the end
smoke of an outrage smearing the sullen sun
dark dusts from Zion trouble the splitting air
ashen the fallen olives in the bulldozed groves
ashen the captive corpses under their crusting blood
bitter ash of Qana and this is not the end

Bitter lees of Qana, you will drink it in the end
ashes of your fury a film on the glass
leaves lifted in the updraft from the violence of the blast
pages of the book that are severed from the spine
scattered on the waters you will taste them to the last
bitter lees of Qana, you will drink it in the end

III

Cedar of Lebanon
    pitched torch against the sky
such fragrance foregone
    in a column of fire

honey soured with cinders
    burns in the throat
sweet milk of murder
    curdles your spit

all your look needs now
    is its cigarette
face drawn from the front
    in night-stained flesh

an eye scoured with ashes
    undone with seeing

The Olive Net

I

Kennst du das Land wo die Olivenbäume bluhen?

Where are you now, gone in the mist,
        gone in the mist of your seine net?

I am you, when I am I.
Together with me recall the sky of Paris.

We went to Aden ahead of our dreams. The moon was shining
        on the wing of a crow. We gazed at the sea.

Eyes:
            shining with the rain that poured
                    when God bade me drink!

I love the rainfall
        on the women of distant meadows.
I love the glittering water and the scent of stone.

We drank rain. Rain we drank.

East of the springs, in a forest of olives,
my father embraced his forsaken shadow.

My mother's hair was never white.

What can we say to the embers of your eyes?
What will absence tell your mother?

You fill up the urns here and feed your heart.

I have a saturated meadow. In the deep horizon of my word,
     I have a moon,
          a bird's sustenance,
               and an immortal olive tree

I am lighter:
in front of strangers I sing:

Kennst du das Land wo die Olivenbäume bluten?

II

March combs its cotton over the almond trees

I gaze upon trees guarding the night from the night
and the sleep of those who would wish me death:

Count the almonds,
        Count, what was bitter and kept you awake

I would break open my shadow
                For the scent of almond
                                to float in a cloud of dust
and grow tired on these slopes.

                                        Come closer and listen.

From the nuts we shell time and we teach it to walk

Ours is a country of words: Talk.
                                        Talk.

                        Let me rest my road against a stone.

It is time the stone made an effort to flower,
The pebble's eyes are not lilies.

        Make me bitter.
                Count me among the almonds.

I will slog over this endless road to its end.

Kennst du das Land wo die Olivenbäume verrotten?

III

God's olive trees rise with the language,
and an azure smoke wafts through this day

I touch the dove's ring and hear flute song in the abandoned fig tree

It still bloomed, as we mixed Yes and No,
A star to burnish our mirrors.

Where should we go after the last border?
Where should the birds fly after the last sky?

see, the land was ours, see,
how we barred the way to the star!

Here or there, our blood will plant olive trees.

Kennst du das Land wo die Olivenbäume ausgerotten werden?

Green as mould is the house of oblivion:
There at last you stepped into the name that is yours.

Here in the final passage.

Where are you now, gone in the olive waters?

We were dead and were able to breathe.

Scarf

Or maybe an invisible scarf had woven itself,
without our noticing, tying us to one another.

—Jean Genet, *Prisoner of Love*

On this day like another
we draw the scarf of many colours
from the heap. How it brings out
the colours in your skirt.

For the killed there is no sheltering
and no talk of it. We do not
speak of the dead gathering
where stillness took over.

I reach for, and can't,
the streaked sand, the figure
of the brother at the door with coffee
the flour on his hands still

The memory of the child
in his mother's lap, blood
sopped, those from whom
all that is human departs

SABRA, SHATILAH, 1982

31

Still There

Mirrorvoir:
    tree version and
        peak dip

sostenuto
    in its silvering—

it is still there
    and it sings—

eye agape
    listening in
the tocsin
    extends its half-life

inwardly falling

Top-freighted pine
                    bends
    earth bound
            star-shook

    a sky-frame arching
        questionwards

    Your arc crooks
        a horizon
    charged
            fraught

    intensest blue
    against the green

An abstract
            smoke
dissipates—

fountain
            flash
frozen:

        momentary branching
                        of the breath
        before the library
                of salt

What next,

        endless

apprenticeship of flame?

17 here, 18 there,

        the sprawled

documents of the dead

Dress the harm fields—

        I drink my water

                from the master's jug:

toxic seepage

            in the clay

all our numbers

            stretched

unbroken

The White Note

What you withhold
        as you speak
lies
        beyond lying

∞

That smile dims
        to a trace
you did not want it
            taken

The red thread
        fades in me
I turn into
        the retaining wall

            ∞

Tell what it takes then
        to be more
the tympanum you are
        enough to resound

Listen, with your multiple ear
into the interval
into the between times
you lean on

∞

The white one
she bends
into the whiteness
the white one

String

        on string

to the white note

                yet

∞

A marked man

        tips the scales

feather breath

        tilts you

War
         is raw law
a meridian
         decides it

         ∞

The dismay of thought
         is history
sway
         of the unforeseen

Ex out
       the name, no
issue grips you
       will less

      ∞

To remember
       to resist
what remains
       goes on, on and off

So much space up inside—
      you hardly knew—
honey combed
      mirror plied

      ∞

A stone song entered
      into the black book
what stands forth
      in the dark room

In the book of names
       is no mourning
without the name
       encrypted

∞

All that remains
       this steel nail
a chink
       on the clinker

Bar Null

All the waves arrive bereft of their refugees,
the trees abolish even their ruins,
amassed in the chamber of zeroes.
There is nothing there to be filled:
you could grow learned in noughts,
study the accumulation of chalk.
That too is waiting, teller of shames
and of dreamwarks, long swells
laid up against dismay, the sack
on your shoulders, slouching downward
off the stone paths, a head full
of brittle figures, relic echoes
on a junkyard of remnants and
refuse: things are the discards
of your philosophy, dismissed,
demented, detained, they drift off
into the half-light, unapt ungrounded.

You carved this voice out of my body, dis-
lodged as if it did not even belong there,
instruments laid out on the table, conductor
of tunings, your one note hangs in the air.
He should have died hereafter, whatever
ever after he took on: these are no fit times
to be dying in, though too many come to,
then and there, their leavings surround us
with our needing. "You know how we live
in two worlds always," so this is written in
divisible ink, as if there might have been
a word for such a time. But he turned a keen
untroubled face home to the instant need
of things, being all abstracted in body, stalled
and forsaken, and then so unwillingly cut
into spirit. Off they go scampering
light-fingered street-wise from the law.

Out of which of the divided skies
will the bird next fly? Across the meridian
the new thing escapes me, there then
not there. After a life of listening
all mixed up with things and things
the night-voice steps your way: yes,
you will die your death, the cypher
imploding inward to the dark and
cosmic quiet. Another sky, another
earth, that is but one condition
of our being, the one annulled
by noughts. They sold all the ashes;
it wasn't enough yet: multiplication
of the deadheads, the most irrational
remains. Rains filled up the jug,
then we guzzled what was left us:
Cry for the bird on the remaindered sky.

How there was always something all edges
asseverating, you have the body it is
the body I want in this gathering of
the querulous. Always we come after
the body that was spirited away, a dense
word cluster tightens the knot in your gut.
Remote and magical dusting takes on
the impress: they keep finding traces
rubbed out, rubbed in, they lift off
the stone with their prints intact,
but still not the thing they want: the want
stays. It may be the want you want,
after all, after the body's been lifted,
after the wanted are rendered into
this afterlife that is the life of things,
something desperately signals the body I want.

Between lovely bluenesses the horizon rules
its edge, listing seawards. All round, blood
in its milk, red moiré, ash grey streaking its
milky silk. It pivots around the standing
stone, pebble dressed, a dot'll do you.
A stone standing along the rim, a pine
cut-out, fog-dodged, determine the limit
you'd meet, a human looming maybe on
the foreshore, a blade opens the distance
jottings shed from its sharp edge
seeding the cloud.
                    Between there and
here it is light that is moving as light
is made to, sky light sea light, ear
enlisted to its wavelength, reduced
to one note rung out, hardly there.

I cast the white stones on the foreshore,
foursquare, loaded with chambered echoes—
like you say, the loss of wind defines
a grave room. Likewise, embers give birth
to the absence of flame: such bearing
will suffer no hurt, easy flow, easy do,
the sovereign is smooth and the run-off
turns no stone, moving others as it will.
Like a blue water clause, scale determines
where you step—beyond the limit
the centre doesn't hold, rhythm grows wily
and makes grooves of its own, will you won't you
one two want to now. We were speaking of
power, showy things and shit: the base is four-
fold and still things move into their refuge.
All along a slow burn festers in the root mat.

By word of mouth or a stone fort opens
its wings to the sea below, below. I
miss you now though there was nothing
between us, only this great null of ocean
an embrasure embraces. A selfie
peeled up from the rock consumes
from the edges: see how it burns!
Round this end of time sense certainty
is circulating, the lone thing taken up
into its sublime abstraction is your con-
cretion or a Jerusalem stone façade redux,
flattened five stories to one, say, such
odds, when the rap comes to your door:
cement dust, ash, blown along the ex corridors.
But to be partial to things, this desert
is full of their traces in the attentive ear.

The voice waves break on the tympanum.
I wanted to net the surf tonight, its
splashy spume falls back from the furl. I was
all set to skim voice traces from the wall
tonight, they were so pressing to my ear,
the frantic orphaned swarm unhiving.
Nothing like you comes back, nothing of your
remains, words dissolving in the acid sea.
An odd leaf falls through radio silence, static
on the air, voices corroding between
the frequencies, snatches of sound dapple
scratching the gap between things. I wanted
to ride every broken wave to the ground
tonight, run interference patterns in the
backwash, waking shattered voices from
the undertow, stories of everything turned to stone.

Silk of self between the lips unspooling
even this nearness, the horizon smear
between blue and deepening blue, a
white-framed rock dashed in the surges,
liquid, liquidating, breaks the series. There
where an island, the stone church, the boulder
stations, older than that, there, the warmath
underbreaks. White underwing riding turbulent
streams, air-fluent, *dem Geier gleich* with
its caustic reflux. News breaks the chain
of evening with its murder of crows, homing,
the thread of memory shreds in the teeth:
ontological cable of this sea-wind heaves
at anchor, messaging madly into the archive.
Line by line, lip service felt in the breath,
leave me just blue enough to thread the eye
of a loop-pole, voice dying from the inside out.

Lightfall deepens into its incendiary edge,
backlit pines define the distance, black steps
across the ridges. Out of the heart of light
a voice speaks, its lidded mouth unseeing.
Hands ensleeved sift the star-salt, the weal
harks back into the time sink, this library
of wax blind to its catalogues of bone,
their scar-lagged proofs. Reserve shifts
across the null places, a whole hand writing
on air, an ember ring tracks it, cutting
the darkness in flight. All his paraphernalia
reversed, its warp order backing up.
Athwart the time I speak, only a breath step
holds him. Straw winds bear down off
the scorched slopes with a faint reminiscence
of ash. Let go. Now is the hour to disperse.

Morning thunder joins the peaks, copula
of rain raises the earth in a bright
snatch of decay. The tenanted house
is mildewed, filming of damp moss sweetens
the granite step. This you must take now,
stone by stolen stone, and tumble: dis-
mantled rock rolling uprooted down the slope.
Seated in solace, bent to his yeasty kieve,
master of fermentations breaks it down: haloes
of wort-rings unfold through the litmus, this
nonsense-mediated decay tense with the ash
of things, raven chatter hectoring the tepid
cloud. I tell you, he found his real face there
down by the sluggish waters, in the dank retort,
till your white head silent and your set jaw
stared everything down into its sullen earth.

A lifeline sutures the hand, crossed, only
that there to read, a seam unseen
fastens the grey graft to the red bark
as an old moon in the young one's lap,
scuzzy aura blurring the scrim. A sheer
wind sings in the breach, damp cinder draught
wafted from the slopes: my dry mouth
tired of its breathing, a white ash
seasons the tongue. Nothing but sky
adds to the sky now a greeny light
diffuses along the crest, ashen light
before the storm. A seeding of droplets
peels from the branch, puckers the sand.
Number and level cyphered my tendered
palm: you might have said dross tide-shunted
at the surfline, wave-crescents fading.

Wave meter paced the shore, keeps time: between
the mountains and the sea, home trudge shrank
into undertow, nil by mouth, lip trap clamped shut,
but still she came ocean-eyed in dream, said see
what I could, see what I knew, see what I was:
the mountain back beyond, holding, weighed down
to this quartz rest—sea-crystal pressed in earth, earth
earth-heavy, clear in the seam light delays in its multi-
shimmering veer. This is the work diverging
from the cast, and your listening-in bone was
all ears to it, to the dream plunged in the earth,
askew to the remembering vase, bud-crested
crystal: from here on in it defines the sill, like
a signature, like an uneasy gaze into refractory
light, with deliberate slowness in the rift loaded
with smithereens, o-mouth to thread at your peril.

Feathered animangel in flight she opens
this articulate assembly, cast out on
the reticent field. A pillar of fire
burns afar, the undressed stone gives back
the day's glare. Mother knuckles dragging
the finest sand for knuckle, clavicle
to string a high note over clinkered earth.
Phosphor drops searing out of the scalded air,
splutter of sparks annulling the bone:
dredged earth laid bare afire, every thing
burns in its own way, with an aura
of hot breath. Dead face turned from me
recedes into the fold, a word breathed in
my ear catches in its knot, reticulate
loops snaring the parting song, this science
of disappearance checking out for now.

Notes

Versions of poems collected here have been published in *Beyond Baroque, Black Box Manifold, Hambone, Irish Anthology of Free Verse, OR: Otis Review*, and *Shearsman Review*. Sequences from this collection have been previously published by Smithereens Press, Magra Books, and Soundeye Pamphlets. Thanks to the editors of all these publications.

Epigraph: Ingeborg Bachmann, "Alle Tage," from *Die Gestundete Zeit / Borrowed Time*, in *Darkness Spoken: The Collected Poems*, trans. Peter Filkins (Brookline, MA: Zephyr Press, 2006): "War is no longer declared / but continued" (translation slightly modified).

"Leavings": a-hain, a-doe, etc: the sequence of numbers in Irish, always preceded in counting by the syllable "a," aspirated before a vowel: *aon, dó, trí, ceathair, cúig, sé, seacht*. We stumbled in numbers.

"Kodalith": Kodalith was one brand name for a high-contrast film commonly used for a brief period in lithography. The resulting negatives are dense black and clear white without mid-tones. They can be exposed in contact with offset-lithography printing plates to an ultraviolet light source to make plates for offset lithography. The combination suggests light writing in stone.

"Arcanum": This work responds to a performance by Fred Moten and Wu Tsang at Greene Exhibitions, Los Angeles, in 2014, in the series *Invito Spectatore: Four Collaborations between Performance*

Artists and Poets, curated by Gerald Maa. It was previously printed in the catalogue for that series.

"The Olive Net" is constructed principally of lines taken from early poems of Paul Celan and from Mahmoud Darwish as translated by Munir Akash and Carolyn Forché. Attempting to translate some of Celan's early poems, I was struck by certain similarities in rhythm and imagery between them and those of Darwish, at least as I knew them in English. I began to imagine a dialogue between the poets, both of whom lived in Paris, though Darwish was exiled there after Celan's death in 1970. As it turns out, Darwish knew Celan's poetry well and even adapts lines from "Marianne," an early poem from *Mohn und Gedächtnis*, in his own "A Cloud from Sodom" in *The Stranger's Bed*. See Angela Neuwirth, "Hebrew Bible and Arabic Poetry: Mahmoud Darwish's Palestine—From Paradise Lost to a Homeland Made of Words," in *Mahmoud Darwish: Exile's Poet. Critical Essays*, ed. Hala Khamis Nassar and Najat Rahman (Northampton, MA: Olive Branch Press, 2008). Some of the affinity between the poets may be explained by their common interest in medieval Andalucia, a centre of shared civilization before the expulsion of both Jews and Muslims from Spain in the fifteenth century. The German refrains are adapted from Goethe's "Mignon's Song," from *Wilhelm Meister*. More than eight hundred thousand Palestinian olive trees have been destroyed in the course of the Israeli occupation and settlement of Palestine.

"Bar Null": Poems from an early draft of *Bar Null* were printed as chapbooks by Archetype, an imprint of Art Center, Pasadena, California. Thanks to Dennis Phillips, Gloria Kondrup, Steve Tusk, and the students in this program for the opportunity to work with them.

With thanks also to Aleister Crowley for the spread and to Robert Kaplan for *The Nothing That Is: A Natural History of Zero*.

GEORGIA REVIEW BOOKS